INTERNATIONAL THEATRE AND CINEMA

EDITED BY HERBERT MARSHALL

THE INDIAN THEATRE

A Kathakali Dancer.

Photo. Paul Popper
Courtesy *Ballet*

Mulk Raj Anand

THE INDIAN THEATRE

Illustrated by Usha Rani

London
DENNIS DOBSON LTD

FIRST PUBLISHED IN GREAT BRITAIN IN MCML
BY DENNIS DOBSON LTD. LONDON

PN
2884
.A6

PRINTED IN GREAT BRITAIN BY
HUNT, BARNARD & CO. LTD. AYLESBURY
232/R

CONTENTS

[5]

THE
INDIAN
THEATRE

THE
POPULAR
THEATRE

A SAFETY CURTAIN, with birds and flowers and buxom Victorian wenches around a fountain, painted in crude commercial colours, bars you from the mystery as you sit in the auditorium. The play begins at about half past ten or eleven, just when you have dozed off after a futile attempt at catching the eye of the lady who sits in the box. For who else but a harlot would think of coming to the theatre at midnight, unattended! Certainly she is much more amen-  able to the whistles, the shrill shouts and the cat-calls of the more experienced roués than to the surreptitious glances of the respectable little man furtively winking to attract her. So you have nothing to do but to chew betel leaf or sleep. Suddenly, there is a rustling and you see through your half open eyes that the safety curtain is going up and also the red plush tabs are parting, followed by the shooting of a gun which somehow miraculously tears a further curtain into two. And there is the clown trying to stand on his head. A thudding fall of his spotted behind and you awaken rubbing your eyes. Your patience with the antics of the clown is rewarded when at last the hero appears singing. He may be representing Sur Das or Hamlet, but he enters singing, dolefully thumping his heart and rolling his eyes as though he were convulsed with the ache of a million broken romances. Gesticulating violently with extended arms, he ultimately reaches a sham balcony and has a vision of the heroine, who opens her arms to receive but not to give; for, instead of coming forward to embrace the hero, she bursts into a dithyrambic song of her own. And thus the play proceeds, slowly, surely, not leaving anything to chance and taking you through the paces, as curtain after curtain opens to the shooting of a gun, by way of comedy, tragedy, farce, heroic drama, morality play, and all just in order to ensure that your education is complete by the time you go home at five o'clock in the morning.

This is by no means an exaggerated account of a performance in one of our rare city theatres, especially if one has the classical repertory of the surviving professional companies in mind. Nothing is too fantastic on this stage. I have been seriously told by a distinguished man of the theatre that during one play a cow was supposed to perform a miracle. She was supposed to enter from one wing of the stage, chew up the rope with which the heroine's hands had been tied by the villain of the piece and then walk out through the opposite wing. Usually the cow performed this trick docilely and efficiently enough, for she had obviously been trained by a circus master. But, occasionally, she took it into her head to walk straight through from one wing to the other without performing the miracle. And on those occasions the manager of the theatre appeared, made a little speech about the perversities of cows and the rarity of miracles, and asked the audience to be indulgent till the cow could be persuaded to come back and do the necessary and that, meanwhile, the heroine would regale the house with a song. Upon

[11]

this the heroine burst out into a melody like a bubul, after which the cow, having been lured back with a bundle of straw, came and duly performed the miracle and walked away, and the play proceeded according to schedule.

In our villages the performance of a play, usually called *Ras* or *Nautanki* or *Tamasha*, though more vigorous and unpretentious, is often a jumble rather like the European revue, consisting of scenes from a religious or a historical play, interspersed with humorous sketches which are based mainly on satirical narratives about the evil landlord, the money-lender or the *Sarkar*, and replete with songs, songs, and more songs. The relieving grace of a village play is that in it we get a simple survival of the most ancient theatrical principle: the players and the audience are one, forming a unity through the circles in which they sit round the improvised booth of the stage while the actors walk up, to and from the dressing room, through the clearing which the audience obligingly affords as and when necessary. Often the audience joins in community singing and the illusion is steadily and surely built up by the actors and the audience acting together, and the spectacle is utterly moving in certain moments. This, however, is not always the case, and the general decay which percolated into our lives through a thousand years of work by codifiers and grammarians of emotions and moods has tarnished the humanity of even the village players. The puritanism of a moribund social order has inhibited the freedom of the mummer, till the taboo against women acting on the village stage is almost complete. In most parts of the country the professional mummers in the village, like the potters or the weavers, form a caste on their own, variously named bhands, nakals and mirasies. They are itinerant players who visit the houses of the peasants on marriage, birth, and festival, regaling the audience with jokes and songs and recitals for which they are paid in kind, but kept at an orthodox distance, being regarded more or less as untouchables.

There are, of course, many self-conscious attempts at the evolution of a new theatrical tradition. For over a hundred years, mostly under the impulse of the Western European drama, foreign and indigenous plays have been written and produced. In Bengal particularly, the genius of the Tagore household gave a definite shape to this art and after the rich creative activity of the last two generations there has emerged a professional stage of a fairly high order. But in

[13]

most other parts of the country theatrical activity is restricted to the annual show of the college dramatic society, usually playing in English to an audience whose own kinetic inheritance is something quite different; and there is the ramshackle circus-theatre of the Parsi entrepreneurs and their imitators.

To such depths of degradation has the great theatrical tradition built up by ancient and classical India sunk! And there seems little hope of redeeming it until we take stock of the whole situation in view of the changes caused by the industrial revolution, and self-consciously select from the remnants of the old tradition those elements which can be synthesized with modern innovations in theatrical art.

THE
FOLK
TRADITION

THERE CAN be no denying that there is a great positive factor in our favour: our people are still possessed by an inordinate love of drama and often display natural histrionic talent of a high order. The presence of this instinct is important. For, in the attempt to mould an art form, the emotional inheritance of the people is important, especially in an art form which draws so largely on the senses.

For drama is organically related to impulse, the quick of life, the throbbing, rhythmic flow of instinct and emotion which gives rise to all movement. The most obvious example of this is in the love-dance of the cock before the hen during the mating season, and the war-dance of the cocks at all seasons. Spreading its bright plumage, panting and blowing but proud, the cock enacts an eternal pageant in the elasticity and beauty of its gait as it prances towards its opponent in the cock-pit. Some mother birds are well known for the way they will walk up and down rhythmically before their nest, if a man happens to be about, in order to guard their little ones.

Perhaps the earliest histrionic efforts of primitive man arose when he disguised himself as a bird or animal in stalking his quarry. Anyhow, the instinct for drama was present long before he became self-conscious, for he seems to have had energy enough to impersonate and represent, coupled with the uncanny assurance that he could move an audience by means of this representation. The power to act was, there-fore, incipient in his nature: the sheer exuberance of his body seems to have prompted him to expand; desire and fear seem to have urged him further, and his growing awareness of the universe obviously enabled him to use this power to extend life and to avert the forces of death.

We do not know exactly at what stage in the development of man the transformation of the dramatic instinct into self-conscious drama took place. But it is fairly certain that an important step was achieved when our primitive ancestors began to dance singly or together, to the accompaniments of their joint cries, grunts and growls, for they could not yet speak or sing. Stamping around the fire, they seem to have been weaving magical spells and in doing this, like M. Jourdain in Molière's play, who talked prose without knowing it, they were initiating the arts of dance, drama and poetry, with the beat of their dancing feet, with their bird-like shrieks and in the magic they were performing.

Specially important in this context is the dance which our primitive ancestors performed before going out to hunt. Some of them dressed up as hunters and the others as the hunted animals, dancing a mimic hunt in which, of course, the hunters invariably won. Those who took the parts of the hunted animals were presumably not directly affected by this wish-fulfilment magical dance, but certainly the hunters began to believe that they were going to kill the animals and generally did succeed in doing so, for they now had the passionate desire to kill that they might have lacked if they had gone out in cold blood. Later on, this mimed hunt became formalized, that is to say certain gestures, sounds and movements were abstracted from the naturalistic representation and developed into symbols and patterns which signified the dance at a higher level.

The same magical idea appeared again when man

began to till the earth and extract his food from it. Certain ritualistic dances were evolved, with rhythmical chants, incantations and spells to make the rain fall and the sun shine so that harvests might grow in profusion. Our ancestors believed that there were spirits behind the mountains, the river, the sky, the rain, the wind, the trees and the earthquakes, gods who had to be appeased with offerings of songs and food, because otherwise they might overwhelm human beings with disasters. These invocations to the good and evil spirits were acted, not by single individuals but by the whole tribe. Many of the hymns in those first books of the world, the Vedas, are pleas to the gods for bigger and better harvests, for an abundance of vegetation and for an increase in fertility all round; and, from a great deal of the later poetry, it is obvious that the tribe danced, enacting the yearly victory of the spring over winter, and to earn blessings, circling like the seasons with an ecstatic intensity such as alone could move the indifferent and exalted gods.

As the tribe danced with a single will, the sheer excitement of rhythm caught their simple imaginations and they were given the joy of their own strength and movement, the joy of creation. And soon if one person showed greater skill in the dance he would step out into the middle and lead the others, while some of those who were tired sat down to take a hand with the drum, or to clap and sing to the beat of the dance, watching the play of words and gestures like an audience. The flow of emotion passed from the actors to the audience and back and gradually it was discovered that some members of the tribe had greater talents than the others in representations of scenes and could stir up emotions in the audience at will, rouse them to love or war or make them laugh. And in the interplay between the actors and the audience the theatre was born.

The skill of the actor seemed to the tribe to have divine origin. Naturally, therefore, the actor began to arrogate to himself the functions of the priest and evolved a symbolism and a technique of which he was the unique custodian, playing to them as well as interceding on their behalf to the gods; and he felt the treble thrill of creating something in himself which was other than himself, communicating it to the audience and to the gods. Once he had tasted this strange power he did not easily relinquish his hold on the community.

But the alteration in the balance of the means of production which took place when the nomadic tribal life yielded to a settled existence, and the other such changes that followed, made men less and less dependent on the gods and gave them a greater belief in themselves and in their own ability to grow their bread and find their water. And the growth of the city state, the nation and world society, enabled man to believe still more firmly that he could shape his own destiny. The gods began to be conceived as made in the image of man rather than the other way about. And the actor began to celebrate the deeds of heroes, of the ideal men in whom the gods had become incarnate. Drama then became personal and concerned itself less and less with the supernatural than with the conflicting good and evil among human beings. And thus the theatre grew, till it

 came to be the commercial art which it is to-day in the great cities of the world.

All the old forms of the drama did not die out, however, but survived in the dances of the primitive tribes; in the ritualistic dances, pageants and tableaux of the temples; in the dances and mimes which celebrate nature myths in our villages; in the enactment

of the heroic deeds of our ancestors through the recitation of romantic narratives as well as in the plays which enact the victory of right over wrong. The *Ras* or *Nautanki,* the *Ram* and *Krishna Lila,* the enactment of the victory of the *Pandus* over the *Kurus,* the *Muharram,* the *Holi* as well as the several harvest dance-dramas, are the apotheosis of the old drama, survivals which are an important reservoir of energy from which a new living art of the theatre can be made. For in India, we have to begin almost at the beginning and come full circle if we are to build up an indigenous tradition rooted in the soil and in the consciousness of our people. They have remained, despite all the civilizing processes they have undergone and despite the sophisticated classical city dramas, the custodians of certain elemental forms. No sudden leap into the future can be attempted, but we can advance only if we develop a national drama rather than a superficial smart middle-class comedy, borrowed from the West.

PURITANISM
AND
DECADENCE

Does this merely mean that the Indian theatre must return to the grunting and howling of the primitive man? Must it resurrect the simple dance dramas of the past and be content with revivalism? No, for we cannot put the clock back even if we wanted to do so. All that is implied here is that we cannot be content to import the smart comedy manufactured in Europe during the machine-age under circumstances very different from those in India to-day. We have to seek inspiration in the vitality of those impulses which have persisted in the sub-conscious strata of our culture. The Indian people have lived close to nature in all the process of history and remained unaffected by the currents which first moulded these impulses into sophisticated forms and then took the decadent form of the classical and city drama of about two thousand years ago.

[23]

Let me develop this point further:

If there is one general fact which may seem to explain the decay of sensibility in the city theatre, it is probably the puritanism which began to seep through the Indian theatre when the medieval codifiers and grammarians dammed the floodgates of creative art by rigid criticism. The soulless formalism with which they tabulated the moods and emotions atrophied those very moods and emotions, and for centuries there has been nothing left to the Indian theatre but the memories and scattered remnants of the classical tradition petrified in the form of the sophisticated drama. But no people can live merely by weeping over the ruins and exalting the graves. Life asserts itself. Certainly, when puritanism and decadence become allied with nihilism and despair born of slavery, and art becomes removed from the people, it needs a change in the social order to create a new art.

It is no use denying that to-day the Indian theatre, as well as the other arts, is looked down upon as somewhat dirty and contaminating, unfit for the sons and daughters (especially the daughters) of respectable middle-class citizens.

Of course, there have been dirty plays and dissolute

players, and the same tradition which ensured the sanctity of the wife, forced the courtesan to provide entertainment. But this perverse morality did not always poison Indian theatrical art. In fact the moral urge, which has now turned sour, supplied the inspiring ideal of the early drama. For, as I have shown above, play-acting began as prayer: our ancestors chanted in unison for plentiful harvests and when they were intent on the resurrection of the King hero and wished to gain immortality. The old drama was thus rooted in ritual and not in entertainment. In its later development the play universally enacted the victory of Life over Death, till the fun of this enactment by itself survived as an aesthetic ideal. Throughout the folk-play, religious observance remained the driving force. And ethical purpose has been most pronounced even in the clowning between the acts of the morality or miracle plays. The actor has for ever been presenting what the people wanted to see, the revenge of evil and the triumph of good. As, however, there can be no showmanship without music, paint, and lights, naturally the pleasure of the senses has remained an integral part of the village theatre; but it is morality none the less. This is so still in Indian folk as well as city drama. For we have come late to industrialism and have not yet evolved an extensive middle class interested, like its European counterpart, in the bedroom farce, and our long struggle against tyranny and oppression has kept art forms closer to the people. As I have insisted, whenever drama has been near the people it has sounded a moral note.

Now, it is obvious to some extent why we must derive enthusiasm from the folk forms, what motifs we should take from them, and how we should develop them self-consciously till we achieve the natural curve of drama from the simplest to the most sophisticated. But it will be easier to understand all this if I take certain surviving folk forms and show exactly how they can be transformed.

THE
ANDHRA
THEATRE

THERE ARE already a number of pioneers of the
theatre who have begun to mould a new tradition
out of the old. A great deal of the dance drama
perfected by Uday Shankar at his Almora centre, as
well as the shadow plays he created after his first
revivals of interest in the dances of India, are cases
in point. *The Rhythm of Life* was, for instance, an
amalgam of motifs taken from the rich storehouse of
people's memory and transformed through the
organization which Shankar had borrowed from
Europe. And much of the work of his colleagues
like Shanti Burdhan in *The Spirit of India* and *India
Immortal* ballets, as well as in the *Holi* and *Ram Lila*
dance plays, owes itself to the principles developed
at Almora. The adaptation by the various language
groups of the Indian People's Theatre Association,
of the ancient *Tamashas* and *Powadas* in Western

[27]

India and the folk forms of Andhra illustrate the same process.

In this context let us take the surviving folk forms of Andhra in South India and see what use has been made of them by the People's Theatre.

The main forms current there were as follows: (1) *Burrakathas* (bardic recitals and folk songs); (2) *Harikatha;* (3) *Veedhi Natakan* (open-air dramas); (4) Regular plays; (5) Choruses.

Burrakathas, or bardic recitals, were the most  popular of all folk forms. The context of these was generally supplied by a racy poetic and prose narrative like the *Ballad of Venkataramani,* the boy who ate his mother's ears. The usual *Burrakatha* group is composed of three people, one of whom is the principal singer. He begins the narrative as a leader, while his two companions supply the chorus effect, all of them using the long Andhra drum as accompaniment. The mode of narration is punctuated by significant pauses in order to heighten the dramatic effect of the story, and the musicians occasionally take a few steps forward, or circle round to the rhythm of the drum at appropriate moments during the narration to emphasize certain emotions or rather to round off certain passages of the story.

During the prolonged decay which marked the history of feudal society when the position of the village bard had become reduced to a mere hanger-on at the nobleman's court, the bardic recital became the heritage of the beggars who went from door to door singing for a bowl of rice. I have had occasion to see how the groups of the Indian People's Theatre Association in Andhra have rescued this form from the ignorant, who practised it as a formula and how, by composing new ballads with fresh social content, they have combined with the natural vigour of the old form a new urgency of conscience, without diminishing any of the gaiety and joy which is inherent in the form itself. I shall never forget how three peasant boys held an audience of thirty thousand citizens of Guntur spellbound up to the early hours of the morning with their recitation of the *Ballad of Venkataramani*, the bad boy who ate his mother's ears. The

[29]

newest ballads composed for *Burrakathas* display a variety of thematic content from the life of the peasants to social reform and the Bengal famine. But the form is specially suitable to the telling of heroic stories.

The traditional use of the *Harikatha* was for the  narration of stories from the epics and the *Pauranas*. Song, prose, poetry and dance were all interwoven by the artist who was called Haridas, servant of Vishnu. The people's theatre groups have taken over several *Haridases* and written up popular themes of everyday life in the convention of the *Harikatha* narrative, thus retaining the purity of the old form but making use of it to extract sympathy from audiences used to the strict metrical verse.

Singing mendicants are a common feature of life in India but they abounded in Andhra, dressed in strange garb, wandering through the land, fortune-telling, selling medicines, diagnosing diseases and generally exhorting people to be good and charitable. Here, as in dealing with other folk forms, the Indian People's Theatre Association has retained the old style but changed the content. Instead of diagnosing bodily ills, the mendicants now diagnose social diseases, prescribe appropriate methods of healing, particularly insisting on an incision here and a major operation there, and rousing the community to action. The fortune-teller now foretells the fate of whole peoples and nations in terms of social analysis. And the mendicant's role is reversed, in so far as now he preaches the social morality of concerted endeavour, and not personal retirement from the problems of the world.

For centuries, *Veedhi Natakam*, or the open-air stage, seems to have been used by itinerant dramatic troupes in the villages of Andhra. But with the coming of modern Western drama with all its paraphernalia of elaborate stage-sets and footlights, the convention fell into disrepute in the eyes of the more snobbish town-dwellers. The taboo was further encouraged by the movies. But, as in the neighbouring Tamilnad where the open-air play

[31]

Teruvukk-kootu was popular the Andhra open-air stage employed a highly developed technique like the *Kathakali* of Malabar, being only less complicated in regard to the make-up of the actors. Now this is forming the basis of the modern play. A play called *Hitler Prabhavam*, the downfall of Hitler, was written in this *Veedhi Natakam* style and was an enormous success. And the Andhra groups have been able to build up a repertory of several plays which have been performed to vast audiences.

Kolatam, the popular folk dance of Andhra, was  like the 'garba' of Gujerat, a vigorous and muscular effort. This, and the more feminine *Lambadi* and *Bathakamma* dances are now being used as the basis of dance dramas and ballets, which retain the costume and the steps of the original but evolve patterns which can awaken the aesthetic emotions at a higher level

Masks used in the Kathakali dance drama.

than was possible to the merely isolated performers of these dances.

The flood of energy which has been unleashed by the improvisation of the ancient village forms to bring joy, enlightenment and amusement to the people by the Andhra theatre, has rendered possible an enormous output of new writing, and no cultural festival is complete in that part of the country without its extensive repertoire. These shows afford inspiration and joy to thousands who had nothing but the drab routine of the open field to fill their lives.

To me the energy and seriousness with which the Andhra Indian People's Theatre Association have transformed their folk-forms is an example of what could be done in the other linguistic zones. I say this because I found a return to reality in the Andhra improvisations which was not merely in the excellence of the mimed execution, but in the impression that it gave me of being completely integrated with the life and tradition of the region. They have not yet been so successful in the recitation of dramatic poetry, for they have not yet worked out how much visible presentation is essential during the narration of a poem. Nevertheless, they give promise of a vital theatre in what they have already done.

THE
BENGALI
THEATRE

THE REGIONAL theatre which has gone a great deal further towards realizing a true synthesis of old and new forms, without actually reviving the old folk theatre, is in Bengal. This is something of a paradox since Bengal had a much richer folk tradition than any other part of India. However, it was the first part of the country to be ruled by the British, and the enactment of the Permanent Settlement Act in 1795 created a new class of absentee landlord popularly known as the Bhadra log. These gentry almost lost touch with the peasantry, the reservoir of folk culture. As in politics, so in the arts, Bengal, therefore, developed a highly talented city culture, located mostly in Calcutta. And this culture was most easily influenced by the West, especially as the British government initiated an educational system based on a foreign language, and propagated the legend of the superiority of Europe in everything, to the detriment of the Indian tradition.

Already before the battle of Plassey, an English theatre was in existence in Calcutta, and Warren Hastings is mentioned as one of its subscribers. At this Calcutta theatre sparkling comedies like *The School for Scandal* and *The Beaux Stratagem* were staged under the direction of one Mr Massinck, said to have been sent out to India by David Garrick himself. At first the female roles were taken by men, but following the example set by Mrs Bristow, women were later introduced. Apart from the English, only the rich native landlords were admitted to the portals of this holy of holies.

Similar English theatres were founded variously by a Russian adventurer named Herasim Lebedeff, by Prof. Hayman Wilson and others, and English classics, mainly Shakespeare and the eighteenth-century dramatists, were presented to the rich Indians.

Under the influence of these theatres, the landed gentry of Bengal gave private shows of which one of the first was the popular medieval drama *Vidyasunder*, enacted by a cast of women as well as men, in the house of Nabinchandra Basu in Sham Bazar.

After this, the idea of applying European stage

[36]

conventions to indigenous material spread and the amateur theatre flourished, fed mostly on English and Indian classics. Some attempt was made at a synthesis. In the opening scene, for instance, it was not the manager, but the *nata* (actor) and a *nati* (actress) who appeared, to deliver a kind of prologue to the play, and the scenic representation was improvised in a form which was symbolic rather than realistic.

The exalted private theatres, lavishly financed by the gentry, flourished, and original plays on the English model began to be written, like *Is this Civilization?* by Michael Madhusudan Datta.

Girischchander Ghosh launched a regular National Theatre in 1872 with a professional company. And many of the later theatres like "The Star", "The Minerva", "The Manmohan" were modelled on Ghosh's effort. The repertory of these theatres included Pauranic plays, rewritten to suit new conditions, adaptations from Shakespeare, historical and social plays. And highly skilful writing began to be produced, such as the plays of Dvijendralal Ray and Rabindra Nath Tagore.

In spite of the deep inroads made by the foreigners into the lives of the Bengali middle class, the intelligentsia reacted sharply against the rulers and led the movement for national self awareness until the end of the first world war when the Gujerati middle class led by M. K. Gandhi wrested the leadership of the struggle. As a result, the upper classes of Bengal were able to resurrect their own language, their dress, their habits of life and traditions. Rabindra Nath Tagore, whose life work as a writer coincided with these developments, went further than most in his dramas to emancipate himself, and by implication Bengali literature, from the spurious and mechanical influences of English forms. He consciously evolved a highly developed, technically efficient style of his own in dramatic writing which owed not a little to the folk culture of Bengal. But a great deal of the fantasy and poetry which he brought to his playwriting was peculiar to a detached individual whose experience of life was limited and highly abstracted because of rigid clan affiliation, and this was betrayed by his poetic narrative and conceptual thinking.

The one great contribution of the British had been the opening of well-equipped theatres in Calcutta. And here, apart from Shakespeare, who enjoyed a great vogue in the many adaptations of his plays into Bengali, the work of many indigenous dramatists was enacted. But the themes continued to be taken from the old Pauranic stories with an occasional dash of the revue-cum-tragedy-cum-farce-cum-opera which reflected contemporary manners and customs. Towards the early years of the twentieth century, however, the social revolt was already in the offing. And it had its repurcussion on the arts in the production of plays like *Nildarpan* on the conditions in the Indigo plantations of Eastern India.

The tradition of the Bengali middle-class stage, therefore, was the only theatrical vehicle in Bengal until just before the beginning of the second world war when a strong wave of anti-fascism was rising. It was, however, during the war that the merging of the Progressive Writers' Movement with the Indian People's Theatre Association in Bengal led to a new orientation of theatrical art.

In 1944 was produced the play *Homeopathy* written by Manoranjan Bhattacharya, a professional actor and a dramatist of distinction. And in the same bill was Bijon Bhattacharya's *Jahandandhi*, together with the poem entitled *Madhubanshir Goli* by Jyotirendra Moitra.

It was the Bengal famine which shook the whole country that produced the greatest spurt of theatrical activity in Bengal. Under the stress of this exigency was produced a play *Navanna* which will remain a landmark in the history of the Indian theatre, for the extraordinary heights it touched as sheer art, the perfection of scenery, costume, acting and the general organization having coalesced to produce lasting memories and a deep stirring in the country.

Navanna (*New Harvest*), was written by Bijon Bhattacharya and produced by the author in collaboration with Shambu Mitra, with the assistance of Manoranjan Bhattacharya and Gour Ghose. The theme of the play, which is in four acts, is the life of a Bengali peasant during the harrowing famine when three million died from starvation and disease. The critic of the Amrit Bazar Patrika wrote about its first performance: 'Nothing can be more topical and therefore more difficult of artistic treatment, especially in the form of a dramatic performance as a famine. For the first time since Dinabandhu Mitra's *Nildarpan* a truly peasant drama has come upon the Bengal stage.' Another paper said: 'This is the real picture of the people —the underdogs in the background of the August Movement, flood, famine and epidemic. It is not to be praised for its novelty alone —its value lies in its capacity to create a sense of fellow feeling for suffering humanity.' The play was

performed before large audiences not only in Calcutta, but in the Mofussil areas and invitations poured
in from the countryside because all the artists were
not in a position to leave Calcutta for more than a
day or two at the most.

The last sentence taken from a report about
Navanna is significant, however, of the problem
which faces the Bengali theatre: It is primarily a city
stage without much connection with the villages,
except that in this particular play, as in Jyotirendra
Moitra's song drama *Navajibaner Gan* (*Songs of New
Life*), the theme deals with the peasantry. The treatment too was on the whole in the realistic technique
bequeathed to Bengal by the European influence and
did not derive to any extent from that current
indigenous village theatre. Therefore *Navanna* is
rather a *tour de force* than the originator of a new
tradition in drama, for the realistic modern technique
of the city theatre is bound, if it is not informed by
folk feeling, to end up either in sheer naturalism or
in the virtuosity of the sentimental tragi-comedy of
the middle-class theatre. An emphasis on technique
as such, as in the American and English theatre,
leaves one with the feeling that all the energy of
electricians, costumiers, property men and set de-

signers, is of no avail if the core of the theatre is neglected, that is to say if there is no living contact between the actors and the audience which in the cities has been dulled by cynicism and snobbery. In my opinion only a constant return to folk feeling which is rooted in the real life of our peoples, can bring a genuine sense of reality to the Indian stage.

The Bengal movement is reorganizing itself in this matter. For they have given a few performances in the *Kabi Ladai* form of recital. In this, a band of village poets with folk instruments like the drum, form opposite parties and wage wordy duels with one another, the leaders of the two bands composing impromptu verses and discussing subjects of moral import. It is possible to use this form, as the Andhra Indian People's Theatre Association has done in dialogues on topics of burning importance, and to develop the humorous as well as the rhythmic possibilities of these bands as a chorus effect, by weaving them into the modern play.

THE
MARHATTI THEATRE
IN BOMBAY

THE NEXT most highly developed theatre in India was that in the Marhatti language which arose mainly in Poona and Bombay. Like the Bengali stage it began mainly under British influence but soon emancipated itself and established a considerable repertoire, which is good literature as well as fair theatre. Beginning with Vishnupanth Bhave, who used amorous and tragic themes, a number of experimental plays were written which rationalized the old medieval performance and led to the formation of the professional Bhave company. They were followed by the Aryoddharaka Company in Poona, the Mahrashtra Company and the Shanunagaravasi Company. The repertoire of these ventures was the mixed grill preferred in the early theatres of Bengal. But if it is remembered that Marhatti power was still a dominant feature of Western India till the middle of the nineteenth century, one can see how the Marhatti

stage became soon imbued with national self awareness. Historical plays about the famous Marhatti
heroes from Shivaji downwards began to be written
and presented. As these were banned, the Marhatti
dramatists invented subtle stratagems to present their
point of view in allegorical fantasies or in farcical
comedies. And there was evolved the humorous
social play, a speciality of the Maharashtra stage. Later,
under the influence of Ibsen and Shaw, Mama Varerkar
wrote social plays in a realistic style where a synthesis
between European convention and Indian content
was attempted. As a leading contemporary dramatist,
Varerkar gave a tremendous lead to the younger
groups which have been re-creating the Maharashtra
village theatre through the *Powada* and the *Tamasha*.

Under the impulse of these vital actors a Marhatti
worker wrote a play called *Dada*. He portrayed in
this piece the day-to-day life of the Bombay workers,
their sufferings, hardships and frustrations with an
authenticity born of grim experience and with a
humanity characteristic of his class. The audiences
were thrilled to see their own everyday lives put
before them so clearly and seemed to be deeply
moved by the realization that they could alter the
conditions of their lives through their own strength.

THE PARSIS
AND THE
GUJERATI THEATRE

THE EXAMPLE of Bhave had greatly influenced the
Parsi community in Bombay. Rich, talented and
easily adaptable, because of the lack of a cultural
tradition of their own, the Parsis took up both
Gujerati drama and the Hindustani stage. The
essentially practical bent of their mind, however,
put commercial success above artistic achievement
and they soon succeeded in vulgarizing every theatrical effort. That they produced men with a rich
histrionic talent there is no doubt, but the lack of a
language of their own made it impossible for them to
develop drama which could survive the years. And
yet they occupied the centre of the theatrical life of
India for more than half a century, with the Alfred,
Madan and Balliwala Companies, performing, mainly
in Hindustan, plays which were either adaptations
from Shakespeare or amalgams of socio-historical-

musical content, and which petered out in the bathetic, decadent displays of the imitators of these imitating Parsis.

The real Gujerati theatre arose, however, as a reaction to the Parsi vulgarity.

Ranachodbhai Udayaram was disgusted with the low *pot-pourri* presented in the Parsi owned and run theatres of Bombay and began to render and adapt the Sanskrit classics. He wrote a popular play called *Harischchandra* and then a social tragedy. After him a school-teacher called Narottam started an amateur company and then three business men founded the Gujerati Company. Later there arose the Bombay Gujerati Company of Dayashanker with performances of *The Morbi of Oza* and *The Doshi* of Dahyabnai Dholsha through whom the modern Gujerati stage arose.

The fact, however, that the Gujerati middle class is mainly commercialist led them, after a little while, to ape the Parsi vulgarians and the new ventures ran through the gamut of pseudo-historical Pauranic and English adaptations to ultra-romantic thrills and ended in the low social farce. Under the weight of all this sensationalism it is a relief to come across the naïve plays of K. M. Munshi who had a ready pen and attacked corrupt social practices. Unfortunately, however, there is a lack of intensity in Munshi's writing, and his vagaries as a politician have brought his literary work into contempt among the public. Mrs Munshi's one-act plays are, on the contrary, much admired, both for their sincerity and polished writing.

C. C. Mehta, a highly talented Gujerati dramatist, has gone much further than any other writer in his linguistic group in bringing into the written play the kind of idiom and technique which may perfect the modern Gujerati drama. His play on the life of the railway workers, *Ag-Gari*, has become an important piece in the repertory of the *avant-garde* theatre. Mehta has a very thorough grasp of technique, and particularly influenced by his knowledge of the radio play he can juggle with his theme, mixing tears with laughter and suspense, through his intense awareness of people. And he deliberately sets out to instruct and moralize in the Shavian manner as in his play on the life of the Gujerati poet, Narmad. But the popularity of his plays among the low priced seats in the auditorium shows that he writes through an alliance with common moods, for nowhere in the world can one touch the core of the pit unless one is instinctively connected with human emotions. Certainly, he has done more than any writer to resurrect the drama from the abject servility of the Gujeratis to the upper middle-class culture of Bengal by a return to the living experience of the Western Indian. Furthermore, he seems to have taken Goethe's advice:

"He who would work for the stage should study the stage . . ."

THE
HINDUSTANI
THEATRE

An attempt towards a Hindustani theatre was made by Imanat who wrote his play *Indar Sabha* at the behest of Wajid Ali Shah, the Nawab of Oudh and enacted it at his court with the Nawab in the main role. Ever since then, however, the disruption created by the British impact on India which inhibited the growth of the theatre in other languages, strangled it in the areas wherever it arose.

Actually, the situation in the Hindustani speaking zones was potentially a very fruitful one. For, although a great many other arts had flourished at the courts of the Great Moguls, the theatre never enjoyed any vogue there, because of the general Islamic taboo against the recreation of human form on the stage which is interpreted as usurping the functions of the Divine creator, the progenitor of the world. Only in the villages, among the peasantry,

[49]

the pageantry of the garland of festivals which decorates the year, both Hindu and Muhammadan, kept the folk forms of *Nautanki* and *Ras* alive. The poet Imanat seems to have drawn very largely on this, but no other dramatist arose who could express the consciousness of a destiny which soars above circumstances through facing them.

The Parsis, who recreated the Hindustani stage, though starting under the impulse of Imanat's *Indar Sabha* and the copious adaptations of the Elizabethans, soon made the theatre purely a business proposition. The Balliwala, Alfred and the New Alfred Theatrical Companies of Bombay as well as the Madan Theatre Co. of Calcutta all distinguished themselves by commercializing the theatre on the familiar formula of 'give the public what it wants'. As usual, this meant titillating the people with songs, jokes, *bons mots* and sensation-mongering, using ham actors and the crudest melodrama and generally giving them their money's worth through the chief actress, always a fashionable courtesan. And for two or three generations the main writer of drama remained, apart from the anonymous adapters of Shakespeare, a hack called Aga Hashr Kashmiri, a third-rate poetaster whose stock-in-trade was the blood and thunder melodrama, with a dash of morality sufficient to get into the skin of the four-anna audience and send them home happy and supposedly uplifted.

The pure drama of more sensitive writers like Abdul Halim Sharar, therefore, became more and more literary while the commercial stage merely decayed till the film and the talkie came and sealed its fate for a time.

The more sensitive minds of the younger generation of Hindustani writers could not but be shocked into an awareness of the inexpressible misery of the people who endured foreign rule and feudal and religious impositions. As the development of democracy in the West, and particularly the Russian Revolution, showed that their dreams of a good life for the people were possibilities, they began from their different angles to tackle the overpowering tragedy of Indian life. Thus a new poetry and prose were born, arising from the dejection of the soul, but intent on struggle. Nor were they daunted by the ineffectuality of much of their efforts in a country teeming with disasters. The notion of struggle itself became for these the chief catharsis, the elevating circumstance.

There is no writer under forty to-day who will deny that at one time or another he did not subscribe to the dominant influence of the Progressive Writers' Association which was formed in 1935. The movement which this body generated has released a tremendous amount of poetry and prose in which the conditions of our existence are constantly related to the extreme limit of possibilities.

The mainstream of this movement met the corresponding theatrical current, which had started from very humble beginnings in the Indian People's Theatre founded by Anil de Silva, a young Singhalese woman writer, in Bangalore, but which had matured in the vast network of Indian People's Theatre Association branches all over the country.

The chief language group of the Indian People's Theatre Association is the Hindustani group. And the most consistent writer of this group has been Khwaja Ahmed Abbas, whose chief contribution, a play entitled *Zubeida*, enjoyed a terrific popularity among audiences both in Western and Northern India.

Zubeida is the name of a girl from the United Provinces who is stirred by the dirges of the funeral processions and the spirited songs of the relief workers outside her house to cast away her veil and join the volunteers. She dies, like many other people, through the lack of an anti-cholera vaccine. Abbas made a conscious attempt in this play to unite the public life of processions with their chants and slogans with the private life of the Muslem household, and he tried to create almost a new form of drama very akin to the living newspaper. And I think he demonstrated one way out of the theatrical debacle, that is to say from the peasant play towards the documentary theatre.

The recent productions of adaptations based on Gogol's *Inspector General* and the Irish play *Remembered Forever* (*Desh Bhagat*) were highly successful efforts in tapping the real emotions of Indian audiences, with their incipient reserves of laughter in the face of the extraordinary anachronisms of our society.

But by far the greatest contribution to the Hindustani stage has surely been made in recent years by the actor-producer Prithvi Raj Kapoor with his two productions *Deewar* and *Pathan*.

With an uncanny theatrical instinct Prithvi Raj seized upon certain memories of his village life as it was presented in the *Ras* of North West India and, uniting several motifs of the folk play, he has knit them into the framework of two modern plays dealing with a contemporary theme, communalism.

Deewar describes in a fabulous form the transition

from the good life of the old India to the misery which the foreign invaders brought into our lives and the wretchedness which was perpetuated in our land by their divide and rule tactics. Here two brothers, who lived happily with the whole village community, are gradually estranged and ultimately a division of all the property is forced, signified by the wall which is created to divide the house. This barrier is ultimately destroyed when the peasants revolt against the misery and hunger following the partition, and the two brothers are reunited.

I am afraid that moving as is this play, and a fairly good example of the community spirit informing the three-act drama, the bad stage sets and indifferent costuming destroyed the illusion to a great extent, though its vitality and urgency was not lost upon people who have been flocking to see it now for almost two years.

But no Hindustani play that I have read or seen has impressed me with its integrity as much as the simple, starkly beautiful and elemental drama of the life on the frontier, entitled *Pathan*.

The story of the friendship between the two families of a Khan and a Hindu nobleman portrays the deathless loyalty which is the essence of the code

of honour in this part of the world, even as the exaction of the ultimate penalty by those who have a feud with these two families shows the evil inherent in this relentless society. The tenderness of the relations between the two households, and in their relations with their servants and re-
tainers during birth, marriage, and death, is unfolded in a pageant which is al-most documentary in its realism. A cer-tain romanticism creeps in through the implied love for the

graces of the feudal life which are contrasted to the new commercial values. This contrast was more explicit in Prithvi Raj's earlier production *Deewar*.

The rhythm of the play is slow, especially in the beginning, but that was perhaps inevitable in an attempt to portray a simple life. It depends less on action or the interplay of wit than on the vigour and authenticity of the characters. But, throughout, with its beautiful setting in the little castle home of the Khan (what a terrific improvement on the sets of *Deewar!*) a subtle doom is immanent and built up through inevitable progression from happiness to tears, to the climax of disaster. The audience knows as it becomes involved in the talk and the sports of this household, its piety and its good sense as well as its follies, that the beautiful life cannot last. And Nemesis comes surely when the Khan sacrifices his own son to appease the enemies of his friend the Hindu nobleman whose son, killing in self-defence, would have been shot by the feudists whose code demanded 'an eye for an eye, a tooth for a tooth'.

The point which I want to make, however, is that although the battle between good and evil is only implied, and society takes its victim, this play is a morality. And yet in so far as evil prospers and the good characters suffer as victims of God's justice this drama is reminiscent of the Elizabethan stage. But it is modern in that certain characters question the Mullah's interpretation of the religious code and even challenge the traditions of the old society by insisting on education. Altogether, *Pathan* stands with the Bengali play, *Navanna*, at the cross-roads of the old and the new traditions, and it is equally revolutionary in that it presents our Indian life with an anxious

regard for aesthetic values which brooks no compromise with the tawdry habiliments of the shows of the Balliwala theatre.

It is noteworthy that, because Prithvi Raj has an instinct for life, he does not fall a prey to the slick American influences which many of our smart-alecs regard as the be-all and end-all of the theatre. Rather, he instinctively writes on political and social struggles which are not considered 'box-office' on Broadway and Shaftesbury Avenue. Politics are part of Prithvi Raj's ethics and the courage with which he goes straight to the heart of the conflict makes his productions a not insignificant part of our struggle for cultural emancipation.

The irony of the theatrical situation in India is however shown by the fact that the second biggest city in India cannot provide a theatre for its pioneer actor-producer. After all the agony of his battle for this art, Prithvi Raj Kapoor can only give three morning shows at the Opera House over the weekends.

Nevertheless, his productions have given a great fillip to theatrical life among the middle classes, while the younger Indian People's Theatre Association groups have helped by taking simpler forms of drama from the peasantry to whom they give performances.

It is this dual programme that may build the ground-work for a theatrical tradition in India. For the theatre must go to the middle classes, garbed in a parody of their costume and manners to show how ridiculous they are. The theatre must go to the poor dressed as the poor and lift them up with their own cries till their calamities become articulate, and compel a change in this sad world of ours.

I feel that that is a truth which applies everywhere. For, not only do the peculiar exigencies of India require the conservation of the two main techniques which appeal to the two chief strata of the population, but the synthesis of the two will bring us to the basis of a new kind of theatrical expression. The community technique of the folk theatre, which may be impossible to re-create in its old form, could nevertheless be used to revitalize the three-act European form. The community spirit could be revived so that drama could become a joint effort of the actors and the audience. Thus may be built a theatre which Lope de Vega had in mind when he wrote: 'The company . . . was like some faces, not a perfect feature in it, but, because of the harmony with which they are united, the face is beautiful'.

[59]

There is no lack of inspiration in the remnants of the broken tradition of our theatre. The place and educational value of drama in soul culture always seems to have been recognized in India. Training of the emotions and control of the body were aimed at. The actor deliberately handled and expressed feelings and emotions, and in the process his body became the vehicle of certain moods, often remaining self-possessed and unaffected. A clear intellectual perception enabled the actor to display emotions without being affected by them and so he learned to cope with them when they occurred in actual life. Now, though India cannot gain much by reviving the formalism of the ancient theatre, it is likely that we will gain enormously by inquiring into its old craft of comedy, tragedy, farce, and the morality play.

As we adapt our knowledge of the survivals of the old folk theatre to the needs of to-day, it is possible that a new indigenous tradition of the Indian theatre may be built which is unique to our country and which may contribute something different to the hackneyed forms current in the contemporary European theatre.

This book is set in 14 pt. Aldine Bembo, a type-face modelled on the fifteenth century letter first used by the Venetian printer Aldus Manutius (1450–1515). Aldine Bembo was cut by Francesco Griffo of Bologna and was used for the first time in a small book by Pietro Bembo, entitled 'De Aetna'. The original design is the earliest of the so-called Old Face types.

In designing the face, Francesco Griffo departed in several important particulars from earlier Venetian models. The ascending letters, b, d, f, h, and l are slightly higher than the capitals. The lower case e has a vertical stroke, a form now preponderant. The italic letters cut to be used with Aldine Bembo are based on the design of the calligrapher Lodovico degli Arrighi, called Vincentino, who became a printer in Rome from 1523 to 1527.

Aldine Bembo, as used in this book, is a revival by the Monotype Corporation from whose matrices it is cast.